Luck and Fortune

Why do I write on this subject?

I felt like writing although normally people don't like writings from guys like me - as I am not well read, highly accomplished, variedly experienced or a celebrity or the like - but I experienced some strange and mysterious things in life, which, may be, very unfortunate people can only have the privilege of having. So I write.

According to me the definition of good fortune is: one who enjoys good health, has the physical and mental capabilities of achieving his goals in life, has good appearance, has happiness in mind and is not prone to accidents…I think such a person can be called a fortunate person. Whether anyone believes me or not, I have learnt from this life that each person is born with a balance of fortune or misfortune. I understood that sum total of a man's personality and life, depends upon three factors: one: GENETIC FACTOR, two: ENVIRONMENT FACTOR and three: HARDWORK FACTOR. And all these three factors are not in one's hand. One cannot take birth with good genetic qualities of one's choice. One cannot as a child arrange a good environment for himself. He lives where he is born, in his family and goes to the school where his parents put him into and plays with such kids who are available. Ability to work hard also depends upon his genetic qualities and environments like his aptitude, attitude, health, nutrition, and motivation and may be many other factors. But all such factors are not his choice but he has to live with them as 'chance' grants him. So this chance is luck or fortune and some are fortunate and some are not fortunate.

So the question is why some are fortunate and some are not. What can be done to become fortunate…I have found the answer and so I write?

I was born with very bad health. I suffered from congenital nystagmus, due to which I never enjoyed a normal vision. I suffered from hormonal misbalance in brain. Hormone called serotonin remained in abnormally lesser quantity in my brain due to which I suffered from acute lack of mental concentration, lethargy, lack of memory and also from chronic depression. My parents were refugees and not quite educated. My dad worked as a soldier in the Indian Air Force and earned a meager salary. My normal body resistance was also poor and I constantly suffered from various kinds of infections. Hence could not do well in studies, games or in any other social activities, as the diseases I suffered from had no cure. So I call myself unfortunate. Because I felt I was unfortunate, I always searched answer to the question why is somebody is fortunate and why is somebody not?

My search went on. I even meditated for hours everyday and searched within to get the answer. After more than 34 years of search, I got some answers and so I write…

I started getting some answers…

Reading was almost impossible for me. With eye problem – congenital nystagmus – it was very slow and after sometime painful. And with hormonal misbalance of serotonin, mental concentration, retention and understanding were horrible. I was also constantly disturbed by unknown memories of war between armies and the soldiers of both sides were Indians and I had regular dreams of such kind. I was shown to a few doctors for my eye problem but they could not be of any help. So I was an utter failure in all the activities of life. Life was miserable. No one knew how I could be helped. My parents were not religious. My father did not practice any religious norms regularly and my mother merely carried out routine worships that she had learnt from her parents. But somehow I came to know that there is something called God who is all-powerful and can help anyone. So not knowing what I was doing, I started praying fervently everyday for months and months. One day while meditating I got a clue that if I start running in the morning everyday then my condition would improve. Somehow I shook my lethargy and got up in the morning next day and went for running. I kept running for next few days in the morning. One day, strangely I felt better, mentally and physically and I found I was able to understand so many simple things, which were riddles earlier. I was feeling free from lethargy. I was able speak with confidence and was cheerful in mind. Depression was gone. During this time reading was much easier as I was able to understand quite a few things. But my nystagmus of eyes remained. But prayer and meditation became a part of my daily life. I also tried to do running and exercise regularly. Within a week I found with distress that my mental and physical condition that had magically improved once again became what it was. Again depression, poor understanding, no concentration, lethargy and all that. It was then I understood that I am having some physical illness that needs medical attention. Strangely after a week or so, again I started feeling fine, no depression, no problems of concentration or understanding etc. I was around 20 years of age at that time. I consulted a doctor who listened patiently and told me that it was all a psychological problem and I must change my thinking habits. He also prescribed some pills, which did not work. So I continued my running and exercise, prayers and meditation. Days passed by and I used to feel fine for a week of so and remained unwell for another week or so. During the time I felt fine, I tried to study and do as many things a possible because of available mental and physical efficiency. But prayers and meditation became a regular habit.

I started learning languages better and was also able learn bit of math. I started reading magazines and newspaper as well. The overall quality of my personality improved quite a bit. It was then someday I was clearly able to feel that there exists an eternal power which people call God, who is all powerful, friendly and wants to help the world. So my habit of prayer and meditation became more and more intense. And I started getting more and more clues and answers…

I got number of clues and answers and one of the most interesting clues that I got was that the *mind is not the function of brain.* Memory, intelligence, knowledge and attitude are not in brain. But they exist forever in an intangible form within an intangible being which may be called *soul.* It is an amazing storage system, which cannot be burnt, stolen, corrupted, infected with virus, pirated or crashed and it has unlimited storage space and serves for infinite time. Probably God collects data from all the souls. Soul is not a matter or energy. It cannot be touched, weighed or destroyed. It cannot be contained. A soul remains in contact with a body so long as the body remains alive. When body becomes unfit to remain alive the soul departs it and again comes in contact with a new body. Human brain only reads and reflects the soul to the extent it is normally capable of. Soul contains vast database of information. Soul has all the information; knowledge and wisdom of all the bodies it has been in contact with in the past with cent percent completeness and accuracy. But the body that is in contact with it now, can normally retrieve only the information that has been stored during the time this body remained in contact with the soul. Memory and wisdom does not lie in cerebrum or cerebellum or in the central nervous system as normally believed. In extraordinary cases soul is capable of networking with other souls and can also retrieve or read data from other souls. Not necessary that soul always contacts a human body only. It contacts all kinds of living beings. Only specialty of a soul, when it is in contact with a human body is, it enjoys some independence and liberty of action. Animals and other non-human living beings do not have that privilege. They are simply programmed in their respective DNAs and their life cycle materializes as programmed. In human beings, with the *power of will*, the programmed life cycle can be altered to some extent. So the human activities are not pre determined and options are available for choosing a better activity to some extent.

Each soul goes through evolution process. Some souls are superior in quality of intelligence than others. Soul when departs a body, carries with it all the experience of the body and when contacts a new body, that new body although cannot have access to all the experiences of the soul which it had in its contact with the previous body/bodies, but unconsciously, however, the knowledge that soul has accumulated in its previous contacts manifests through the new body. The great scientists, inventors, prodigious children and philosophers are examples as they are superior species of evolution.

Soul is very possessive about the body it is in contact with and remains with it as long as achievable. But when the body is no longer fit to live, the soul departs to find a new body as per it qualifies to deserve. After departing a human body, if the soul does not deserve a human body, it has to contact a non-human body like that of an animal or may be even reptile. These are all cycles of fortune and misfortune. It is after millions of reincarnations, a soul finds a human body, which gives it the independence and liberty of choosing activities in life. A soul during its contact with a human body, if attains perfection in its purity, it does not require to reincarnate. This soul then mingles with the eternal soul – the Almighty – forever. Further, soul not only carries the memory and experience of previous lives forever, but also carries the balance of fortune it has earned or lost during lifetime. Negative balance of fortune, if carried over, the new life would be full of misery. One can develop negative balance in one's lifetime as well, although he may have been born with a positive balance of fortune if he exhausts his balance by bad deeds. In that case he would start suffering misfortune in that life itself.

Whatever I have realized about soul and mentioned above cannot be proved scientifically but I beg to challenge any scientist or physician or a rationalist to prove otherwise.

I also got the clue as to what fortune and misfortune are. Every human being is born with a credit or debit balance of fortune. Anyone who is born with a massive credit balance of fortune enjoys life tremendously. That person is blessed with very good health, good looks and lots of wealth, mental and physical abilities to achieve his goals and enjoys happiness of mind and is not prone to accidents. A person born with massive debit balance of fortune, suffers ill health, is poverty stricken is mentally and physically incapable of achieving his goals in life, does not have happiness in mind and is prone to accidents. It is something like this. The soul carries with it the credit or debit balances of fortune like memory and experience.

Credit balance of fortune can be increased during one's life and can be wasted as well.

However, a person can endeavour to increase his credit balance of fortune. How? I have got that clue also. I am revealing the answers one by one.

Answer one:

One who does all his legitimate duties prudently, completely and honestly increases his credit balance of fortune and one, who does not, decreases his balance of fortune, **because God deputes every soul with human body for some purpose**. Hence, one must try to keep oneself fit to perform his duties successfully.

We all want to function at the best level of efficiency, both physically and mentally. And many of us know heart by heart that we are not doing so as certain elements are preventing us from leading the kind of life we *really want to lead*, within the available resources. That is to say, we are not making the best use of our available resources and the elements that come in the way to our functioning at the best possible manner, are also not unknown to us altogether, but we do not find ourselves strong enough to see them with an open eye and take measures for their elimination. In a way, we are escaping from the reality. That is to say, we are failing in one of our duties in life.

Let us, nevertheless, try to examine, what elements prevent us from functioning at our best. The elements are: worries, ill health, depression, fear, sorrows, regrets and such other undesirable feelings.

There is *only one reason* for our worries, anxieties, ill health, depression, sorrows, fear and any other undesirable feelings and that is: *failure to perform our legitimate duties*. One who performs all his duties properly and completely is a blessed individual and has no sorrows in life. Let us examine this fact closely; A school child, whose duty is to study his lessons and complete his home work, if does not perform them, has all the problems in the world, when he goes to school next day. He worries; he suffers and sometime undergoes punishments. An employee, who does not perform his work properly, has problems from the employer, results in worries, anxiety, reprisals and sometime loss of employment. If the parents do not perform their duty towards their children, then children get spoilt and give them all the sorrows of world. And if one does not perform the duty of taking reasonable and prudent care of one's health, then again he has all the problems. Thus, there is not even a streak of doubt left that all our problems, worries, sorrows, unhappiness stems from only one reason and that is: **failure to perform the legitimate duties prudently and completely**.

Duties that apply to almost all of us are:

1. Duties towards oneself e.g. taking due care of one's health and hygiene etc;
2. Duty towards others, i.e. family, relatives, friends and society as a whole;

3. Duty towards one's job/occupation/profession etc. and
4. Duty to maintain good human relationship with all people who come in touch or contact.

While talking of duties, let us remember the magic maxim:

"Wisdom knows what to perform,
Skill knows how to perform,
And virtue performs it."

Above formula, to attain happiness and to function at the best appears very simple. Yes, indeed it is quite simple. All problems stem from failure to perform one's duties. Why then one fails at all? One fails to perform one's duties only owing to either one or more of the following reasons:

1. **LETHARGY;**
2. **FEAR AND**
3. **MISCONCEPTION.**

In life, we all have tasted failure sometime or the other. It really tastes bad. If we analyze, as to why did we fail, the answer would be either the failure was directly or indirectly attributable to fear or lethargy or some kind of inherent misconception. How then can one remove these three evils from one's system – the lethargy, the fear and the misconception? Quite simple – there are only two requirements:

1. Unity of thought, speech and action and
2. Faith in the system of universe or nature (or whatever one may call) or the Supreme Power.

Let us discuss these two requirements in a better detail:

Unity of though, speech and action: When one fails, what one usually says? One says, failure is due to some reasons beyond his control. He looks for excuses. He blames either others or circumstances or sometime his fate. But he never comes out with the real reason for his failure that is his lethargy, fear or misconception. But in his inner judgment, he knows the real reason – he knows that the failure is because of one or more of the three evils in his system – lethargy, fear or misconception. So there is no *unity of thought and speech.*

Instead, if one makes an honest confession regarding the reasons of one's failure, one makes a psychological gain out of it. When one confesses one's weaknesses honestly and openly before others, one automatically builds up a *mental resistance within*, against those particular weaknesses. The chances then become lesser for him to repeat such failures due to those particular reasons, which he has openly confessed before others. Thereby, his power of will becomes stronger and stronger and the weaknesses like fear or lethargy or even misconception, which are basically mental blocks, start diminishing gradually and in course of time, they even get eliminated. The Bible says: 'confess your sins and repent'. These ancient words still hold good in modern times. Thus in this manner, one develops *unity of thought and speech*. Thereafter, having confessed that real reason for one's failure, one should then think and declare as to what actions should be taken so as not to recur failure again and immediately start *working* on them. Thus, there will be *complete unity of thought, speech and action*. The result will not be gradually.. One has to constantly hammer and forge in order to build up a stronger character. Then sooner or later, one will realize that 'the failures are really the pillars of successes'.

Faith in the system of universe or nature (or whatever one may call) or Supreme Power: Some people find it difficult to believe in the existence of a Supernatural Power that governs the marvel of entire universal system. They argue that the whole system of universe, the solar system, life cycle, all creations of nature's wonders are all a mere chance and that no supernatural power is governing all these. They are the people without faith. People without faith are at tremendous psychological disadvantage, as they constantly suffer from an inner feeling of insecurity. May be there are a few exceptional individuals, who are although non believers and yet they are of strong characters and are quite successful in life. But decidedly, such individuals are negligible in number. The main reason for their success, if examined, would be perhaps, their conscientious performance of all their duties. But the fact remains: 'exceptions do not prove the rule'.

The greatest scientist of 20th century, Albert Einstein had said: 'God is not playing at dice'. He had said this after making a detailed examination of the physical laws that govern the universe. He had realized that the whole system of universe is so meticulously planned, with foresight of millions of years, which is possible only by an intellect of supernatural kind.

Many years before, I had read some part of a book, written by an American author named Dale Carnegie, which had helped me a lot and I had jotted down that part of the book in a piece of paper, which I am rewriting below.

"Those days are gone, when people debated about the conflict between science and faith in Almighty. One of the most modern sciences, the Psychiatry, is teaching what the ancient holy books taught. Because psychiatrists know by research that prayer and a strong faith in Almighty will banish the worries, anxieties, the strains and fears that cause more than half our ills. Dr. A. A. Brill, an American psychiatrist said: 'Anyone who is truly religious does not develop a neurosis'."

Mahatma Gandhi had confessed: 'without prayers, I should have been a lunatic long ago'. Dr. Alexis Larrel, who was honored with Nobel Prize, said in a Reader's Digest article 'Prayer is the most powerful form of energy one can generate. It is a force as real as terrestrial gravity. As a physician, I have seen men; after all other therapy had failed, lifted out of disease and melancholy, by the serene effort of prayer – prayer like radium is a source of luminous self-generating energy – in prayer human beings seek to augment their finite energy by addressing themselves to the infinite source of all energy. When we pray, we link ourselves with the inexhaustible motive power that spins the universe. We pray that a part of this power be apportioned to our needs. Even in asking human deficiencies are filled and we arise strengthened and repaired - whenever we address God in fervent prayer, we change both soul and body for the better. It could not happen that any man or woman could pray for a single moment without some good result;'

Therefore, should we not accept a belief in God, because we need such belief? Call it God or Allah or Paramishwar – why dispute with definition as long as the mysterious powers of nature take us in hand.

If one does not know how to pray, then one should just sit down in a comfortable posture, close the eyes and take little deep breathing through nose, so as to attain a composed state of mind. Then with faith in the potency of Almighty say in mind the following words: 'O ruler of this gigantic universe, bless me with your love, so that I remain happy and comfortable. Give me courage instead of fear, make me dynamic instead of lethargic and make me clearly understand so as to remove all my misconceptions, so that I perform all my legitimate duties properly and completely'. While aspiring to perform our legitimate duties, we should not become *'duty crazy'* and so at the same time also remember the following prayer:

"God give me courage to change what I can;
Serenity to accept what I cannot change;
And the wisdom to know the difference."

Regular prayer of this kind automatically transforms one in to a stronger character, his abilities, his power of will and determination enhances day by day. Magical effect of prayer becomes visible sooner than one can imagine.

Leading a systematic life: Having mastered the above principles, one should then try to make his day-to-day life a little more systematic. After all, the essence of life is performance of one's duties. And one can perform his duty only at *present*, and not in the past or in future. Therefore, the concentration should be on present day – TODAY. If we live perfectly today – *only today* – because we cannot possibly live perfectly in yesterdays or in tomorrows – then our yesterdays become perfectly lived ones, and there is every hope that our tomorrows shall also be well lived. Therefore, prepare for TODAY.

One should make a Master list of all the tasks and duties that one thinks has to be performed in one's life. Then each morning, he should see the list and make few additions, if found required. Then the list for TODAY should be prepared i.e. out of the Master list, which of the tasks that can possibly be accomplished today and required to be performed today, should be listed and then GO AHEAD AND ACCOMPLISH THEM. Next morning again review the Master list, delete the items that have been accomplished, add if any new items come in mind and then prepare the TODAY'S LIST and so on. This practice does not require much time but on the contrary saves lot of time and confusion, because one knows clearly what is required to be done TODAY ONLY.

So to conclude, let us all function well, perform well and lead a blessed and enjoyable life.

I feel, the political leaders are born with massive balances of fortune. Most of them are not performing their duties honestly and sincerely and yet they are enjoying life. But as per my realization they are steadily exhausting their balances of fortune and they may end up very unfortunate or may be reborn as very unfortunate or their off springs may have to pay the price. I humbly beg to suggest them to try honestly to do their best for the people.

Answer two

We must try to maintain the credit balance of fortune, which may diminish if we do not follow the rules of Eternal Soul – the Almighty.

So the second answer that I got in this regard is that we must not hurt any soul. We hurt a soul and we get a debit entry in our fortune balance. And when we make a soul happy, we get a credit entry in our fortune balance. It is not quite difficult to understand as how can we make a soul happy or unhappy. Give food to a hungry person, we make a soul happy. Treat well and we make the soul happy. Insult a person, we make a soul unhappy.

Scientists are doing great job to make many souls happy. They invent new drugs, which heal sick people. They are inventing new gadgets that give comfort and happiness to people and also solve their problems. So are physicians, teachers and so many such people engaged in the services of mankind? Even without being a scientist or a physician, one can give happiness to souls. So many poverty stricken people are seen all around. Try to give them bit of food, clothing and shelter, according to your capability. Give people right information that can benefit them. When you work in your office, do you really help people when they come to you? What I have seen in many government, public utility offices and courts, the clerks sitting in such offices, try to harass people as much as possible to extract bribe. And their officers are also least bothered as they are busy in their own ulterior motives.

They don't know how quickly they are exhausting their balances of fortune.

Soldiers have to kill at times while performing their duty and if such killing were done purely out of duty, as not avoidable, then would not amount to a debit entry in fortune balance. Same soldier, in times of natural calamity, gets the opportunity to help people in distress. Judges have to pronounce even death sentences and punishments but that is performance of legitimate duty and does not amount to any debit entry but a credit entry when done with full honesty.

Making a soul happy is one of the easiest ways to increase the balance of fortune but most people waste their balance of fortune by hurting and hating people.

It is quite easy to remain fortunate indeed.

Answer three

Another simple answer that I got for reducing balance of misfortune or increasing the balance of fortune is: be truthful always. Being truthful means, not only telling the truth but also be honest, refrain from doing anything dishonest, harmful, adulterating, damaging etc. Some industries are making money by making spurious drugs. Some are making baby food, which are made from cheap and harmful material. Now people have even started making artificial milk, called the synthetic milk. Also illegal weapons are being made used for criminal acts and all these are done for making money. People for fulfilling needs and to get happiness and satisfaction in life require money. But this kind of money diminishes fortune balance and misfortune is not far away, because credit balance of fortune is not inexhaustible. Life is not as short as we think. Misfortune may strike in this life itself and if not, all balances of fortune and misfortune are carried forward with meticulous accuracy to next body that your soul shall be in contact with.

So don't cheat, don't defraud and don't commit a crime. And also don't be arrogant.

It sounds difficult to remain absolutely truthful. Try for sometime and see what happens. Nobody will starve to death or be destroyed by cruel world, if one is truthful, as most people think. In this very world, there are numerous people who are truthful and also good to others. At least I don't find any of these kinds of people suffering in any way going by my definition of 'fortune'.

My life started with great misery and by believing and adopting these answers, I am quite a happy person now. I am leading reasonably decent life and I have never lost anything by being truthful.

Anyone is welcome to verify the facts in my case.

Answer four

A soul, when attains perfection in its purity, does not require contacting a new body. Such soul mingles with the Eternal Soul - we call the Almighty.

How can a soul attain perfection in its purity? Simple. Anyone who performs all his legitimate duties to the best of his ability, prudently, honestly and completely and never hurts any soul, instead makes other souls happy and is completely truthful is a soul in its perfect purity. He is equal to God. God is the king of Universe - none can reach beyond that height.

All that I have written may appear like a fairy tale to many because there is no immediate and tangible evidence available in their support. Therefore, do not believe blindly all what I have written, instead, practice for a month at least and figure it out for yourself – 'what you gain or what you lose'?

Phone: +919839204783
E-mail: sirkar@rediffmail.com
ALL ARE WELCOME TO CONTACT ME…

Useful links:
➢ http://www.parapsychology.org/
➢ http://www.med.virginia.edu/
➢ http://reincarnationcafe.com
➢ http://allfaith.com/Mystory/drea m.html
➢ http://www.allexperts.com/ep/32 84-103382/Reincarnation/SUMIT-KUMAR-SIRKAR.htm

<u>My Address</u>

Flat No. 73, Ratan Mahal,
Civil Lines,
Kanpur 208001,
India

Please record your personal experiences here, if you want to
Practice the principles as advocated in this book:

_____
_____
_____
_____
_____
_____
_____
_____
_____
_____
_____
_____
_____
_____
_____
_____
_____
_____
_____
_____
_____
_____
_____
_____
_____
_____
_____
_____
_____
_____
_____
_____
_____
_____
_____

www.ingramcontent.com/pod-product-compliance
Lightning Source LLC
Chambersburg PA
CBHW050350290526
45785CB00006B/2715